A Pillar Box Red Publication

in association with

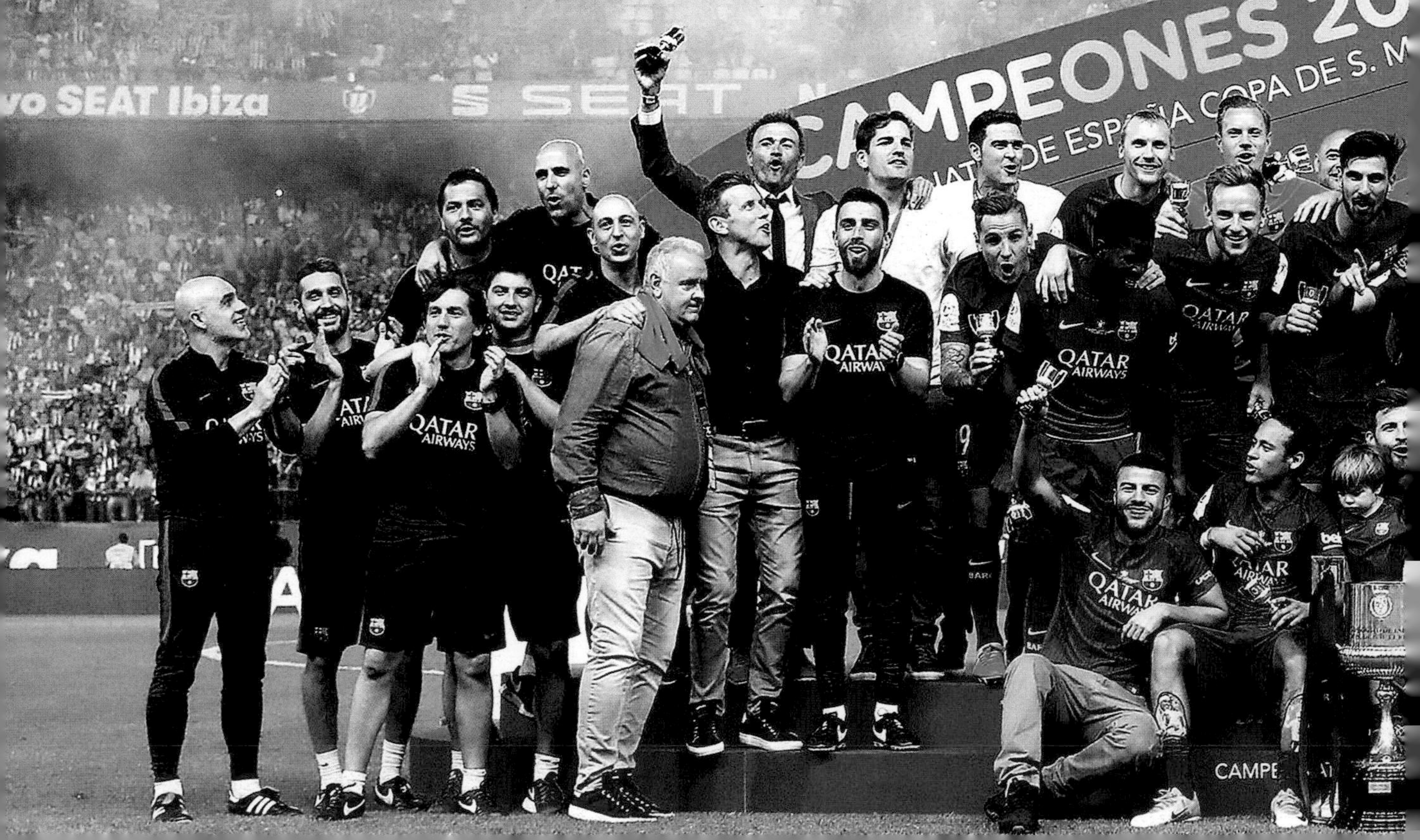

BARCELONA ANNUAL 2018

Written by
Stephen Fishlock, Jamie Evans & Ben Wier

Designed by
Darryl Tooth & Calum Booth

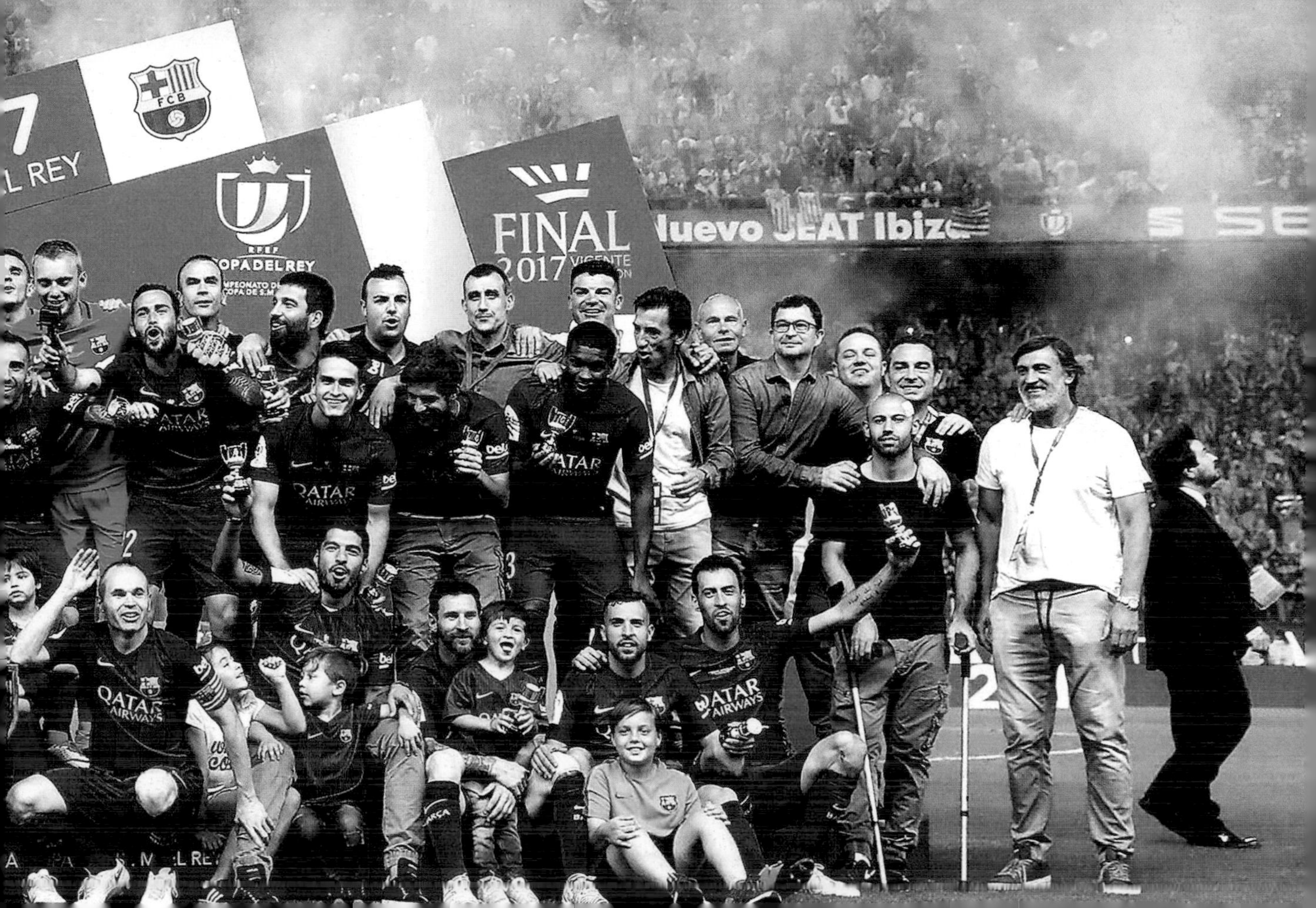

CONTENTS

MESSI
500 GOALS

Last season, LIONEL MESSI hit his 500th goal for BARCELONA! Take a look at some of the best and most important strikes of his career...

Barcelona	2	0	Albacete

May, 2005 When a young prospect was introduced to the Nou Camp pitch in the 88th minute of this game towards the end of the season, nobody realised they were about to witness history! Within seconds, Messi had raced on to a chipped pass from Ronaldinho, lifted the ball over the keeper and scored his first Barça goal.

GOAL 2

| Barcelona | 5 | 0 | Panathinaikos |

November, 2005 Messi had to wait six months for his next Barcelona goal, but it proved to be another crucial milestone. After a mix-up in the Panathinaikos defence, the little Argentina wing wizard saw his opportunity to delicately chip the ball over the goalkeeper, and calmly slot in his first of many Champions League goals.

GOAL 14
GOAL 15
GOAL 16

| Barcelona | 3 | 3 | Real Madrid |

March, 2007 While Messi's reputation in Spain was already big, he exploded onto the world stage with his first goals in El Clasico. Having already equalised twice for his team, he stole a point in the dying moments, with a bursting run and rocket shot past Iker Casillas.

GOAL 19

| Barcelona | 5 | 2 | Getafe |

April, 2007 Possibly Messi's best ever Barcelona goal came in this Copa del Rey semi-final clash. Leo was compared to Argentina legend Diego Maradona after dribbling the ball from the halfway line all the way through the entire Getafe defence – just as Maradona had done against England at the 1986 World Cup!

GOAL 77
GOAL 78

| Real Madrid | 2 | 6 | Barcelona |

May, 2009 As well as being one of the best Clasico performances ever, this was a key game for Messi. For the first time, Pep Guardiola swapped him with Samuel Eto'o and used him in the centre as a 'false nine' – and it worked perfectly. His brace at The Bernabeu marked the start of the most prolific period of his career.

| Barcelona | 2 | 0 | Man. United |

May, 2009 The first of many final head-to-heads between Messi and Cristiano Ronaldo was won by Leo. Before the game, the Barcelona star had been accused of being too small, ineffective in big games and poor against English sides. But his header sealed his second Champions League trophy and silenced his critics.

GOAL 80

GOAL 171

GOAL 172

GOAL 178

GOAL 179

Barcelona	3	1	Arsenal

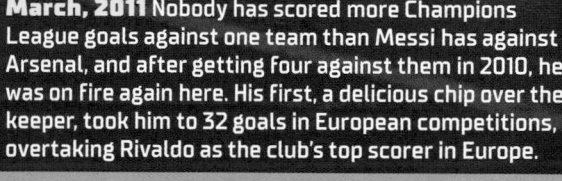

March, 2011 Nobody has scored more Champions League goals against one team than Messi has against Arsenal, and after getting four against them in 2010, he was on fire again here. His first, a delicious chip over the keeper, took him to 32 goals in European competitions, overtaking Rivaldo as the club's top scorer in Europe.

Real Madrid	0	2	Barcelona

April, 2011 The 2011 CL semi-final threw up the clash the whole world wanted to see, but Messi stole the show. After poaching his first at the near post, his second was pure genius. He played a one-two with Sergio Busquets on the halfway line, then ran through the heart of the Real defence before sliding the ball past Iker Casillas.

GOAL 224

GOAL 225

GOAL 226

GOAL 227

GOAL 228

Barcelona	3	1	Man. United

May, 2011 In a repeat of the 2009 Champions League Final, Barcelona were totally dominant at Wembley. Wayne Rooney's goal had made it 1-1 before half-time, but then Messi took over. After his surging run and left-footed shot from outside the box, there was no coming back as Barcelona cruised to another CL title.

GOAL 180

MESSI SPECIALS

Messi's scored some spectacular goals in his time. Check out the pick of his epic wondergoals...

Barcelona	3
Valencia	0

GOAL 109 **March, 2010** Messi's first Puskas award nomination came after this moment of magic. The ball seemed attached to his feet as he dribbled right through the defence to score!

Real Zaragoza	2
Barcelona	4

GOAL 113 **March, 2010** When Leo collected the ball just inside Zaragoza's half, there didn't seem to be much danger. Seconds later, he'd left a trail of defenders in his wake and ripped the net!

Atletico Madrid	1
Barcelona	2

GOAL 223 **February, 2012** This is possibly the best free-kick of Messi's career! From a tough angle more suited to a right-footer, Leo clipped it over GK Thibaut Courtois and sealed a late win.

Barcelona 4 | 0 Espanyol

May, 2012 With only two games of the season left to play, Messi's chances of becoming the first player to score 50 La Liga goals in one season looked slim. Two penalties, a free-kick and an ace finish later, Leo was celebrating another record against Barça's city rivals.

GOAL 249

GOAL 250

GOAL 251

GOAL 252

GOAL 282

GOAL 283

Real Betis 1 | 2 Barcelona

December, 2012 After a remarkable 2012, Leo broke an incredible 30-year record in Seville. His two goals took him past Germany and Bayern Munich legend Gerd Muller's record of 85 goals in a calendar year, and by New Year's Day he'd extended the record to 91!

Barcelona 4 | 2 Real Betis

May, 2013 Six months later, the same team were on the receiving end of Messi on a mission again, as he set another phenomenal record. His two goals at the Nou Camp meant that he'd scored in 21 consecutive La Liga matches – a run which included a ridiculous 33 goals!

GOAL 312

GOAL 313

Barcelona 7 | 1 B. Leverkusen

March, 2012 Another record was toppled here when Messi became the first player to score five times in a single Champions League game. In one of his best ever individual displays, the little genius was unstoppable as he fired his team to the quarter-final stage.

| Athletic Bilbao | 2 |
| Barcelona | 2 |

GOAL 311

April, 2013 The footwork that Messi showed to hold on to the ball under pressure from three markers was absolutely incredible, and the ice-cool slotted finish was even better.

| Getafe | 0 |
| Barcelona | 2 |

GOAL 331

January, 2014 The victims of Leo's first great solo strike suffered at his hands again in the Copa del Rey, as he waltzed through the defence and around the keeper to net.

| Barcelona | 5 |
| Espanyol | 0 |

GOAL 453

May, 2016 Another stunning free-kick not only made Messi the joint highest scorer in the history of the Catalan derby, it also moved Barça to within one win of their 24th title.

GOAL 345

GOAL 346

GOAL 347

Barcelona 5 | 1 **Sevilla**

November, 2014 In MSN's second start together at the Nou Camp, Leo showed he was still the main man – even with those two world-class strikers alongside him. Another epic hat-trick took him to 253 La Liga goals, and clear of Telmo Zarra as the league's all-time top scorer!

GOAL 366

GOAL 367

GOAL 368

Real Madrid 3 | 4 **Barcelona**

March, 2014 Two penalties fired Barça to a dramatic late win here, as Messi became only the second player, along with Ferenc Puskas, to score two Clasico hat-tricks. In doing so, he overtook Real Madrid legend Alfredo Di Stefano as the fixture's all-time top goalscorer.

Barcelona 3 | 0 **Bayern Munich**

May, 2015 Ahead of his return to the Nou Camp, former manager Pep Guardiola said Messi was 'too good' – and so he proved with two quality goals in this semi-final. After drilling in the opener with his left foot, Messi left World Cup winning-defender Jerome Boateng on the floor, before chipping Manuel Neuer with his right.

GOAL 406

GOAL 407

Athletic Bilbao 1 | 3 **Barcelona**

May, 2015 Messi's first goal in the 2015 Copa del Rey Final was voted the second best net-buster of the year in FIFA's Puskas award. Surrounded by loads of Athletic Bilbao players on the right wing, he wriggled through four or five challenges on his way to slotting the ball home to seal part two of Barça's historic 2015 treble.

GOAL 411

GOAL 412

GOAL STATS!

Get a load of the mind-blowing stats behind Messi's 500 Barcelona goals...

HOW?
22 Header
2 Other
74 Right Foot
402 Left Foot

WHEN?
1 Extra Time
222 First Half
277 Second Half

TYPE?
25 Free-Kicks
60 Penalties
411 Open Play

WHERE?
73 Outside Penalty Area
427 Inside Penalty Area

GOAL 413

GOAL 414

Barcelona	5	4	Sevilla

August, 2015 If there was any doubt about the world's best free-kick taker, Messi ended it with two stunning attempts in the UEFA Super Cup against Spanish rivals Sevilla in Tbilisi. After clipping one over the wall from the edge of the penalty area, Leo stepped it up by bending one in from 25 yards a few minutes later!

GOAL 424

River Plate	0	3	Barcelona

December, 2015 The 2015 FIFA Club World Cup Final saw Messi come up against the team that had scouted him as a boy in Argentina. His clever first-half finish helped Barcelona seal their fifth trophy of 2015, and saw the Argentina legend score in six club competitions in a year for the second time of his career. Legend!

GOAL 500

Real Madrid	2	3	Barcelona

April, 2017 The goal that took Messi to 500 could not have come at a more perfect time. With ten-man Madrid piling forward for a winner, Barça countered. Jordi Alba broke down the left before cutting the ball into a little pocket of space at the edge of the box, where Lionel lashed it home. His iconic shirt-holding celebration will go down as one of football's most famous images.

HOME OR AWAY?

14 Neutral Venues

204 Away

282 Home

WHICH TEAMS?

24 Valencia

29 Sevilla

27 Atletico Madrid

WHICH GOALIES?

17 Iker Casillas

21 Diego Alves

18 Gorka Iraizoz

ASSISTED BY?

31 Xavi

42 Dani Alves

34 Andres Iniesta

WORDSEARCH

Can you find the names of these expensive Barcelona signings?

```
J C W V I Z C V F Z F B O F C P Z K L B Z P F M R K N X L A
U O G L E X M C L V X I E Y C I D L C F Y F R W U M T B E D
R U S E W R A F O X X F X I D N U U A D Z A K J X M J P G E
X U T U K Q B D P J D R T E E E X Z P K D P Q O F K P M K Q
E F J V A K Y J E U Z I R O N A L D I N H O C C R Q L L H M
H T S O M R M M Z I K W S Z U D X A M Z B I N C R G W Q X T
S U N A A J E W M A R H Z D S Q R T I B V N Z S N E J N U V
N R J S N V V Z R I V H G B N R F F G O K L F P U O H W Y E
E A F K N C R I V A L D O T I X E I M B H K V D P V V N Z R
U N E J R F H B B D Z K F V H D K I F H L H A L C A C E R M
W I O C B A I E B P P L G Z W D H H S J M G D M R N X Y T A
G L Y V T C C A Z I V U E M M A X A G L B R F A L N L C F E
U P S F E T O I M Y U I F U R I E N G P A V J S X I Y T S L
Y M V V P R P L K V Z V R B G N L J C M E S N C J L B M K E
G E T O O A M K O S M E I J O Q J I Y P W G J H S C F W G N
F W E I U P R A T J S R J R M N N E T I R Q T E R E Q O M W
D L L H T I S V R U R T R O E U N M T O V L W R R X W Z B Z
Z P S B A I D T Z S J M M M S S S G M D C M G A V V H P X O
Y K S F E K L Q L O S U R S V Y F M A W O C C N X Q D Z N B
T P D O K A T H S A L D K K Q K O O T P J P H O Q E Z F T F
T S F Y C O H I G R O G L N Y C Z V H N K B Y X T V N I K W
X R L I V M A E M Q Y M N Z E J O E I P J R G I O J P B H X
Z U A D P R R N S I J B E D B N M S E Y M B R O P S C T F K
W B L U P B S K Q X O C C O R N F D U M F I Y E Q X G U V N
X Y V O A W S O A B S A V I O L A T R V T G N J P N G K T U
H T E F C D X F N D A H S B M W J X O E I H S Y L Q Y V B Q
T W S P D L D S H G K G E P C X T X O M C D K A A A M U D G
K J K V N U F T B R S L O N Y Y P K O D T S I M Z M U F V B
B J B V I L L A I V H S I S R X X O W B B L Y M W U S E O R
S F R J M P Y A N D E R S O N Y N J E H B N I L J Q I J T A
```

Alcacer	Fabregas	Kluivert	Overmars	Song
Alves	Geovanni	Lopez	Rakitic	Suarez
Anderson	Gomes	Mascherano	Rivaldo	Turan
Chygrynskiy	Henry	Mathieu	Ronaldinho	Umtiti
Deco	Hleb	Milito	Sanchez	Vermaelen
Eto'o	Ibrahimovic	Neymar	Saviola	Villa

SPOT THE DIFFERENCE

Study these Barcelona v Atletico Madrid pictures carefully, then see if you can find the ten differences between them!

ANSWERS ON PAGE 60

INIESTA
BARCELONA LEGEND

"Remember this day – the day you first played with Andres."

That was how Pep Guardiola described Iniesta when the two players trained together for the first time in 2000. The legendary captain was reaching the end of his playing career with Barcelona when a fresh-faced 16-year-old joined first-team training. Pep was impressed. Turning to Xavi, he said, "You're going to retire me. This lad is going to retire us all." He may not have known that he would go on to manage his young team-mate, but he realised straight away he'd just played with a future Barça legend. What Pep saw that day has since been seen by the whole world – one of the most intelligent footballers to ever play the game. Iniesta's passing and dribbling ability are outstanding, but it is his awareness and vision that have led to him being regarded as one of the greatest midfielders of all time.

THE BEGINNING

Louis van Gaal gave Iniesta his debut v Brugge in the 2002 Champions League, but it wasn't until 2004-05 that he became a regular under Frank Rijkaard. The Dutchman placed great faith in the midfielder, fielding him in all but one game of Barça's title-winning campaign. By the 2006 Champions League Final, he was a key part of the squad, and came off the subs' bench to help beat Arsenal and secure the club's first European trophy since 1997.

GUARDIOLA REUNION

The return of his hero as manager in 2008 took Iniesta's game to a new level. Alongside Sergio Busquets and Xavi, the trio were the perfect midfield for Barça's style. Iniesta's incredible vision and impeccable control made him the mastermind behind the team's attacks, as they won absolutely everything. His last-gasp strike against Chelsea in the Champions League semi-final is still one of Barcelona's most important and dramatic goals ever.

TOP OF THE WORLD

By the time Pep left in 2012, Iniesta had established himself as the world's best midfielder. He scored the winner for Spain in the 2010 World Cup Final, won his third Champions League with a dominant display in 2011, and finished in the top four of Ballon d'Or votes four years straight. His 400th game in a red and blue shirt in April 2012 showed that he was already well on his way to becoming one of Barça and Spain's all-time greats.

CAPTAIN, LEADER, LEGEND

With the retirement of Carles Puyol and the ageing of Xavi, Iniesta took over captain's duties for the 2014-15 season. Once again, he was central to the club's success, and was Man of the Match in the Champo League Final as Barça won another treble. The records have continued to tumble – last season he moved up to second in Barça's list of appearance makers and won his 30th trophy for the club – no player has won more silverware for them.

BARÇA TROPHY CABINET

4x Champions Leagues

8x La Ligas

3x Club World Cups

5x Copas del Rey

3x European Super Cups

7x Spanish Super Cups

NOU CA[MP]

DEVELOPMENT

'The New Field' has seen a number of expansions over the years, peaking for the 1982 World Cup, where the capacity was increased by 22,150 to make room for over 120,000 fans. It is set to be expanded again, and the 'Nou Camp Nou' will be ready in 2021.

Official Name: *Camp Nou*

Capacity: 99,354

Year Built: 1957

First Match: *Barcelona 4-2 Warsaw*
September 24, 1957

Record Crowd: *120,000*
Barcelona 1-0 Juventus
March 5, 1986

SHOWPIECE EVENTS

The Nou Camp has hosted two Champions League
finals – most recently in 1999 when Man. United
lifted the trophy – the opening game of the 1982
World Cup and the 1992 Olympics football final.

SEASON REVIEW

BARCELONA's 2016–17 season was packed with massive wins, loads of goals, drama and silverware! Check it out...

AUGUST

The players celebrate a record 12th Spanish Super Cup

2016–17 kicked off in perfect style for Barça, as they collected their first trophy of the season within the first two games. In a repeat of the UEFA Super Cup and Copa del Rey finals of the season before, they faced Sevilla, chasing their 12th Spanish Super Cup. With Neymar still at the Olympics, Arda Turan took over on the left flank and impressed, bagging an assist and two goals across the two legs, as the club extended their record for Spanish Super Cup wins.

The Turkey winger continued his strong start by scoring six minutes into La Liga's opener with Betis, while Luis Suarez picked up where he left off the previous season too. His hat-trick took him to an incredible run of 17 goals in six league games, as Barça moved straight to the top of the table. The game was to be Chile goalkeeper Claudio Bravo's final appearance for the club, but with Marc-Andre ter Stegen ready to replace him, the defence was in good hands.

BARCELONA'S RESULTS

14/08	SUC	Sevilla	0-2	Barcelona
17/08	SUC	Barcelona	3-0	Sevilla
20/08	PRD	Barcelona	6-2	Real Betis
28/08	PRD	Athletic Bilbao	0-1	Barcelona

SEPTEMBER

It's seventh heaven for Barça against Celtic

Luis Enrique's decision to leave Suarez, Lionel Messi and Andres Iniesta on the bench against Alaves backfired, as Barça suffered their first defeat of the season. It was a different story three days later however, as all three players were on target in the demolition of Celtic. The attack was firing on all cylinders as the first top-of-the-table clash approached against Atletico Madrid. Despite dominating possession, they were unable to kill off the visitors, particularly after Messi hobbled off with an injury on the hour. The Argentine faced three weeks out of action, but in their first test without their star man, Barça showed no signs of missing him. Turan continued his early season form with goals in both Gijon and Gladbach, as Los Cules stayed within touching distance of league leaders Real Madrid at the end of the month.

BARCELONA'S RESULTS

Date	Comp	Home	Score	Away
10/09	PRD	Barcelona	1-2	Alaves
13/09	UCL	Barcelona	7-0	Celtic
17/09	PRD	Leganes	1-5	Barcelona
21/09	PRD	Barcelona	1-1	Atletico Madrid
24/09	PRD	Sporting Gijon	0-5	Barcelona
28/09	UCL	B. M'gladbach	1-2	Barcelona

OCTOBER

Neymar and co. are stunned by Celta

After Real could only draw with Eibar, Barcelona's trip to Celta Vigo gave them the chance to move to the top of La Liga, but Luis Enrique's men failed to take it in spectacular style. Inspired by Iago Aspas, Celta stunned the visitors by racing into a 3-0 lead before half-time, and were in danger of seriously embarrassing them. An unlikely brace from defender Gerard Pique and a Neymar penalty added some respectability, but it was clear that they were badly missing star man Messi.

Fortunately, the No.10 made his return following the international break, scoring just three minutes after appearing off the bench against Deportivo. In his first start back in the team, he faced his former boss on the touchline, and his old team-mate in goal. But an outclassed Pep Guardiola and a red-carded Bravo were powerless to stop another Messi masterclass, as his second Champions League hat-trick of the season moved Barça five points clear of their Group C rivals. His ability to fire his team to victory continued the following weekend, too. With the score in Valencia locked at 2-2 in injury-time, Messi stepped up to bag the winner from the penalty spot, but the three points came at a price. Iniesta had to leave the pitch with a serious knee injury, and with Pique and Jordi Alba already sidelined by knocks, Barça's squad was to be tested.

BARCELONA'S RESULTS

Date	Comp	Home	Score	Away
02/10	PRD	Celta Vigo	4-3	Barcelona
15/10	PRD	Barcelona	4-0	Deportivo
19/10	UCL	Barcelona	4-0	Man. City
22/10	PRD	Valencia	2-3	Barcelona
29/10	PRD	Barcelona	1-0	Granada

NOVEMBER

Suarez celebrates his winner in Seville

Man. City manager Guardiola got revenge against his old side on Barça's return trip to Manchester, yet the Spaniards remained top of their Champions League group ahead of the important league trip to Sevilla the following weekend. After falling behind, Messi once again inspired his team with an equaliser, before Suarez added the winner just after the hour. The win moved them four points ahead of their opponents, but still two behind Real Madrid. After the international break, they failed to close the gap with a goalless draw against nine-man Malaga. Their reliance on Messi was exposed once again, as illness prevented the forward from playing, while Suarez missed out through suspension. Leo returned to net three times in the next two games and help secure top spot in the Champions League, but was rested for the Copa del Rey clash with Hercules. With the first Clasico of the season just around the corner, Enrique took the opportunity to give some young players a run out, and 18-year-old midfielder Carles Alena seized his opportunity with a stunning strike from 25 yards.

Alena sparkles against Hercules

BARCELONA'S RESULTS

Date	Comp	Home	Score	Away
01/11	UCL	Man. City	3-1	Barcelona
06/11	PRD	Sevilla	1-2	Barcelona
19/11	PRD	Barcelona	0-0	Malaga
23/11	UCL	Celtic	0-2	Barcelona
27/11	PRD	Real Sociedad	1-1	Barcelona
30/11	CDR	Hercules	1-1	Barcelona

DECEMBER

Suarez bags the opener in El Clasico

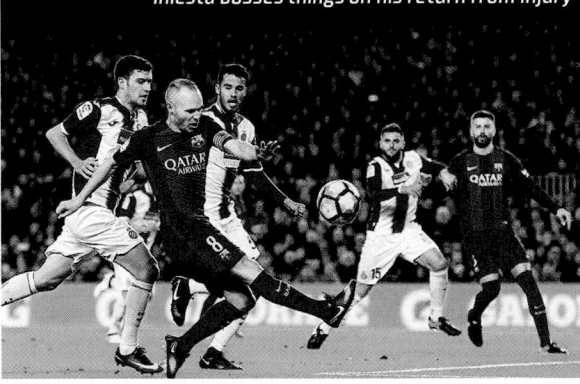
Iniesta bosses things on his return from injury

With Real six points ahead at the top of La Liga, the pressure was all on Barça in the battle between the top two, and they took the lead in the second half through Luis Suarez. In a bad-tempered match which had 35 fouls, the visitors had the last laugh, as Sergio Ramos headed home an injury-time equaliser to maintain the gap at the top.

But Barcelona bounced back to finish the month strongly. Another comfortable win in Europe was backed up by a strong performance against bottom club Osasuna, with Iniesta returning from injury to dominate the midfield. Local rivals Espanyol were swept aside the following weekend, and with the gap at the top cut down to three points, the momentum was building. They ended the year in style, too. A second hat-trick of the month for Arda Turan and Paco Alcacer's first goal for the club gave them a comfortable passage into the next round of the Copa del Rey, where Athletic Bilbao were waiting.

BARCELONA'S RESULTS

Date	Comp	Home	Score	Away
03/12	PRD	Barcelona	1-1	Real Madrid
06/12	UCL	Barcelona	4-0	B. M'gladbach
10/12	PRD	Osasuna	0-3	Barcelona
18/12	PRD	Barcelona	4-1	Espanyol
21/12	CDR	Barcelona	7-0	Hercules

JANUARY

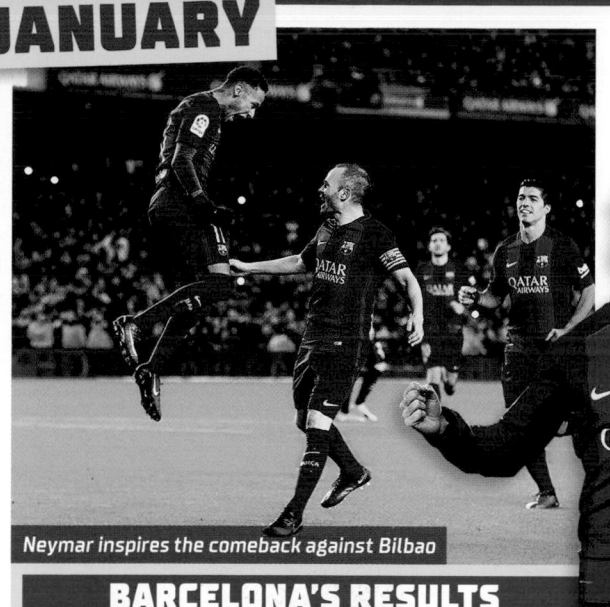

Neymar inspires the comeback against Bilbao

With the Barça players still recovering from the Christmas break, Athletic Bilbao caught them out with a strong performance, taking a 2-0 lead inside the first half. Despite finishing the game with nine players, the hosts held on to take a 2-1 lead into the second leg. The holders' place in the Copa del Rey was in serious danger, yet once again MSN were on hand to fire them through. Suarez's 100th goal for the club and Neymar's cool penalty pegged Bilbao back, and with the game heading for extra-time, Messi struck a quality free-kick from 20 yards to send them through.

After a comfortable win over Las Palmas, Barça were back in the Basque region for the Copa del Rey quarter-finals. Neymar was on target from the penalty spot once again to give them the advantage in the first leg, but it was starlet Denis Suarez who stole the headlines in the second. The young midfielder produced his best performance in a Barça shirt, bagging two neat finishes, and helping to seal a comfortable win to reach the semi-final. Their final game of the month however, was not so easy. A spirited Real Betis side put in an excellent display at the Estadio Benito Villamarin, and only a 90th-minute equaliser from Suarez could rescue a point.

BARCELONA'S RESULTS

05/01	CDR	Athletic Bilbao	2-1	Barcelona
08/01	PRD	Villarreal	1-1	Barcelona
11/01	CDR	Barcelona	3-1	Athletic Bilbao
14/01	PRD	Barcelona	5-0	Las Palmas
19/01	CDR	Real Sociedad	0-1	Barcelona
22/01	PRD	Eibar	0-4	Barcelona
26/01	CDR	Barcelona	5-2	Real Sociedad
29/01	PRD	Real Betis	1-1	Barcelona

FEBRUARY

Messi silences the Vicente Calderon

BARCELONA'S RESULTS

01/02	CDR	Atletico Madrid	1-2	Barcelona
04/02	PRD	Barcelona	3-0	Athletic Bilbao
07/02	CDR	Barcelona	1-1	Atletico Madrid
11/02	PRD	Alaves	0-6	Barcelona
14/02	UCL	PSG	4-0	Barcelona
19/02	PRD	Barcelona	2-1	Leganes
26/02	PRD	Atletico Madrid	1-2	Barcelona

Celta Vigo's surprise victory over Real Madrid in the Copa del Rey quarter-finals gave the semi-final clash between Atletico and Barça extra significance, with the winner expected to go on and lift the trophy. In Atletico's last ever CDR game at the Vicente Calderon, Barça led 2-0 at half-time through Suarez and Messi, but Antoine Griezmann's header gave the hosts some hope ahead of the second leg.

In the action-packed return leg, Suarez was Barcelona's hero with a first-half goal, but by the end of the game he had become the villain. Double yellows for Sergi Roberto and Yannick Carrasco reduced both teams to ten men, and after Atleti pulled a goal back, the Uruguayan was given his marching orders too, ruling him out of the final. Although he made up for his sending off with a brace against Alaves, he was powerless to stop a thrashing in Paris in the CL.

PSG were totally dominant and, despite collecting two La Liga wins to stay within touching distance of Real Madrid, Barça's season was in serious trouble.

PSG thrash Barça

MARCH

Nobody will ever forget the PSG comeback

March began with a big surprise, as Luis Enrique announced that he would be leaving at the end of the season. Faced with the seemingly impossible task of overturning a 4-0 deficit from the first leg against PSG, the coach used his next two league games to experiment with a new attacking formation. Switching to a back three, Barça destroyed Gijon for the second time of the season, before taking their revenge on Celta for their earlier loss. Although they had prepared for PSG, Barça remained big outsiders to make it to the CL quarters, but nobody could have predicted what happened next.

A Suarez strike inside three minutes set them on their way, and while they had luck on their side to go 3-0 up through an own goal and a penalty, an unlikely comeback was on the cards. Edinson Cavani's effort seemed to have killed off the tie, until the final few minutes turned into the Neymar show. Still needing three goals to go through, he scored one of the goals of the tournament by bending an epic free-kick in from 25 yards, and when he added another from the penalty spot three minutes later, victory seemed inevitable. With the whole team thrown forward, an inch-perfect chipped ball from the Brazilian found the boot of Sergi Roberto, sparking wild scenes at the Nou Camp. An amazing night of drama will go down in history as one of Barça's most famous wins, and one of the CL's greatest ever comebacks.

The magic couldn't continue however, and Barça were brought back down to Earth with a disappointing result in Deportivo. Although they improved in the home win over Valencia, they ended March two points behind Real Madrid having played a game more.

BARCELONA'S RESULTS

01/03	PRD	Barcelona	6-1	Sporting Gijon
04/03	PRD	Barcelona	5-0	Celta Vigo
08/03	UCL	Barcelona	6-1	PSG
12/03	PRD	Deportivo	2-1	Barcelona
19/03	PRD	Barcelona	4-2	Valencia

APRIL

Neymar's red card in Malaga saw him banned for El Clasico

BARCELONA'S RESULTS

02/04	PRD	Granada	1-4	Barcelona
05/04	PRD	Barcelona	3-0	Sevilla
08/04	PRD	Malaga	2-0	Barcelona
11/04	UCL	Juventus	3-0	Barcelona
15/04	PRD	Barcelona	3-2	Real Sociedad
19/04	UCL	Barcelona	0-0	Juventus
23/04	PRD	Real Madrid	2-3	Barcelona
26/04	PRD	Barcelona	7-1	Osasuna
29/04	PRD	Espanyol	0-3	Barcelona

A busy April began with two convincing wins to keep the pressure on Real, before they suffered their third away defeat of the season. After former Barça striker Sandro Ramirez had given Malaga the lead, Neymar saw red for two yellow cards, yet a draw in the Madrid derby meant that Barça stayed within touching distance of their title rivals.

Their away form in the Champions League did not improve however, and once again they were totally outclassed – this time by Juventus. After the comeback versus PSG, there was genuine belief the deficit could be overturned in the return leg, but the Italian champions were simply too good. It was with this defeat on their minds that Barça went into El Clasico more determined than ever to retain the title. Goals from Messi and Ivan Rakitic had given Barça a second-half lead, but when James Rodriguez equalised on 85 minutes, the game looked set for another draw. However, with Ramos sent off for a wild tackle, gaps began to open up in the Real defence. Jordi Alba broke away down the left, and picked out Messi perfectly for the record breaker to slot home his 500th Barcelona goal and another Clasico winner. Barça were back on top.

Copa number 29 sparks wild celebrations from Barça's stars

Neymar nets his third Copa final goal in a row

Although their Clasico win and subsequent victories over Osasuna and Espanyol took Barça to the top of La Liga, Real's game in hand meant that the title was still in their hands. With 15 goals in the last five La Liga games of 2016-17, MSN were on fire in the closing stages of the season, as Barça pushed their rivals right down to the wire. A 2-0 win at Malaga for Real on the final day of the season meant the dream of a hat-trick of La Ligas was over for Barcelona, but there was still some silverware to play for.

Bidding to become the first team in over 60 years to win three Copas in a row, Barça produced one of their best displays of the season at the Vicente Calderon against Alaves. Messi, assisted by Neymar, opened the scoring with his 54th goal of the season, before the Brazilian added the second on the stroke of half-time. In the absence of the suspended Suarez, Alcacer sealed the result with a goal to end his debut season in style.

The match was Enrique's final game in charge, as Barcelona said farewell to a legend. Having made 300 appearances and winning plenty of trophies as a player at the club, the former midfielder packed even more into his three seasons as manager. With nine trophies out of a possible 13 on offer, he will go down as one of the most successful coaches in the club's history.

Luis Enrique goes out on a high

BARCELONA'S RESULTS

06/05	PRD	Barcelona	4-1	Villarreal
14/05	PRD	Las Palmas	1-4	Barcelona
21/05	PRD	Barcelona	4-2	Eibar
27/05	CDR	Barcelona	3-1	Alaves

STAT ATTACK!

Get a load of BARÇA's biggest signings, huge trophy cabinet, record goalscorers, Ballon d'Or winners and loads more!

FIVE BIGGEST SIGNINGS

	PLAYER	YEAR	FEE
1	Ousmane Dembele	2017	£135.5m
2	Luis Suarez	2014	£65m
3	Zlatan Ibrahimovic	2009	£57m
4	Neymar	2013	£48.6m
5	Paulinho	2017	£36.4m

FIVE BIGGEST SALES

	PLAYER	YEAR	FEE
1	Neymar	2017	£200m
2	Luis Figo	2000	£37.2m
3	Alexis Sanchez	2014	£35m
4	Cesc Fabregas	2014	£27m
5	Yaya Toure	2010	£24m

MAJOR TROPHIES

5 Champions League

3 FIFA Club World Cup

4 European Cup Winners' Cup

3 Fairs Cup

5 European Super Cup

24 La Liga

29 Copa del Rey

12 Spanish Super Cup

MOST APPEARANCES

Player	Appearances
Xavi 1998-2015	767
Andres Iniesta 2002-	630
Carles Puyol 1999-2014	593
Lionel Messi 2004-	583
Migueli 1973-1989	549
Victor Valdes 2002-2014	535
Carles Rexach 1965-1981	449
Sergio Busquets 2008-	432
Guillermo Amor 1988-1998	421
Andoni Zubizarreta 1986-1994	410

6

Pedro became the first player to score in six different official club competitions in 2009-10 – Messi later repeated the feat!

CHAMPIONS LEAGUE RECORD
ALL-TIME

PLAYED 226

WON 132

LOST 41

DRAWN 53

GOALS 459

CONCEDED 225

9 Barcelona founder Joan Gamper scored nine goals in a single game on three separate occasions between 1901 and 1903 – a club record!

ALL-TIME TOP SCORERS

- Mariano Martin 128
- Rivaldo 130
- Samuel Eto'o 130
- Angel Arocha 134
- Paulino Alcantara 143
- Josep Escola 167
- Josep Samitier 184
- Laszlo Kubala 194
- Cesar 232
- Lionel Messi 507

0 Barcelona are one of only three La Liga clubs – along with Real Madrid and Athletic Bilbao – never to be relegated from La Liga!

11 Number of Barcelona Ballon d'Or winners!

- Luis Suarez 1960
- Johan Cruyff 1973 & 1974
- Hristo Stoichkov 1994
- Rivaldo 1999
- Ronaldinho 2005
- Lionel Messi 2009, 2010, 2011, 2012 & 2015

BIGGEST VICTORIES

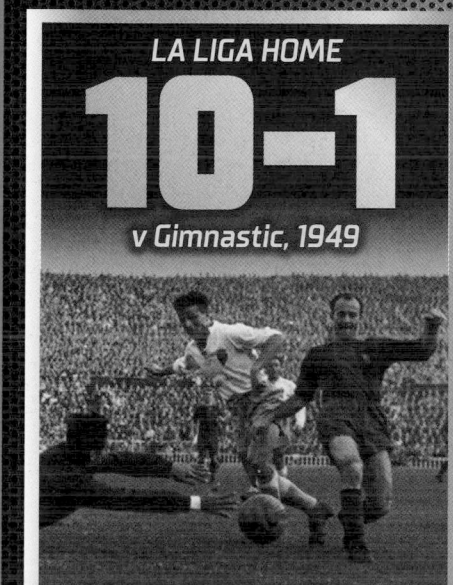

LA LIGA HOME 10-1 v Gimnastic, 1949

LA LIGA AWAY 0-8 v Deportivo, 2016*

*Also beat three other teams 8-0

facebook
103+ MILLION Likes

twitter
23+ MILLION Followers

Stats only include official matches. Correct up to the start of the 2017-18 season.

RAKITIC
MIDFIELD MAESTRO

The man who pulls the strings for the Catalan giants.

One of the most important players in Barcelona's recent history joined back in 2014 for a bargain £18 million. Ivan was already a La Liga superstar with Sevilla, but the move elevated him from a decent CM to one of the best ballers in the world. With him in the engine room, Luis Enrique's team were able to evolve from the Tiki-Taka style that had made them dominant, to a much more fast, incisive style.

With the technical ability of Barça's finest midfield stars, combined with his energy and direct passing, Rakitic has played as big a part in the club's recent success as MSN did. His greatest moment came in the 2015 Champions League Final against Juventus – after a free-flowing move, he was on hand to convert Andres Iniesta's quality cross and send the club on their way to their fifth CL trophy.

XAVI REPLACEMENT

In 2014, Barça began to search for Xavi Hernandez's replacement. The legendary pass master was well into his 30s, and the club needed fresh legs to play alongside Iniesta. The Catalan giants didn't have to look far – Rakitic's form for Sevilla that year had taken them to Europa League glory, and earned him a place in the La Liga Team of the Season. He was the perfect choice!

TREBLE HERO

Barcelona's £18 million man settled into his new team straight away. The Croatia baller's more direct style suited Barça's new-look front three – while Xavi was a patient passer, Rakitic helped the team press higher up the pitch and get the ball to MSN as quickly as possible to work their magic. With this new style of play, Luis Enrique's quality side swept to a mind-blowing treble!

MIDFIELD MASTER

With Xavi leaving the club after that success, and Iniesta's appearances restricted, Rakitic became the team's main man in midfield from 2015. He rose to the challenge perfectly, playing all but two league games of the team's successful La Liga season, and collected another Copa del Rey against his old club Sevilla on top of the Club World Cup bagged earlier in the campaign!

CLASICO STAR

Another Copa del Rey trophy followed in 2016-17, but the highlight of Rakitic's season was definitely a special night at The Bernabeu. After setting up Messi for Barça's first goal, the midfielder curled an absolute peach into the top corner past Keylor Navas in the Real Madrid goal. As a star in one of the most dramatic wins ever, Rakitic wrote himself into Clasico's history books.

RAKITIC'S PASS ACCURACY

2016-17: 85.8%
2015-16: 88.1%
2014-15: 90.6%
2013-14: 79.3%
2012-13: 78.7%

BARCELONA BRAIN-BUSTER!

How well do you know the Spanish giants?

1. In what year did Barcelona legend Andres Iniesta make his senior debut for the club?

2. What nationality is Barça's awesome shot-stopper Marc-Andre ter Stegen?

3. What is the Nou Camp's total stadium capacity – under 90,000 or over 90,000?

4. How many Champions League titles have the club won – three, four or five?

5. Which English club did Barcelona sign goal machine Luis Suarez from in 2014?

6. How many times has a Barcelona player won the Ballon d'Or – 11, 12 or 13?

7. What position does Barcelona hero Rafinha play - full-back, centre-back or midfield?

8. What colour shorts did the La Liga giants wear last season?

9. Which player left Barça for a world-record £200 million in 2017?

10. Who are the club's massive city rivals – Alaves, Espanyol or Osasuna?

1 ....
2 ....
3 ....
4 ....
5 ....
6 ....
7 ....
8 ....
9 ....
10 ....

FACE IN THE CROWD

Can you spot ten current Barcelona superstars in this picture?
The players below are all in the Blaugrana crowd somewhere!

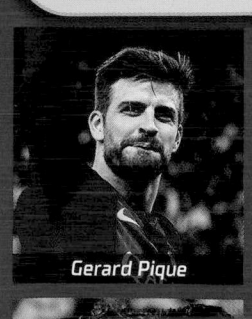
Gerard Pique

Sergio Busquets

Luis Suarez

Lionel Messi

Andres Iniesta

Sergi Roberto

Samuel Umtiti

Andre Gomes

Javier Mascherano

Denis Suarez

ANSWERS ON PAGE 60

LA MASIA'S CURRENT CROP

GERARD PIQUE

Playing alongside Messi in Barça's youth team, Pique's talent was obvious and in 2004, Man. United snapped him up. His form on loan at Real Zaragoza in 2006-07 made Barça determined to re-sign him, and he returned as one of Pep Guardiola's first signings to become one of the best and most decorated defenders ever.

ANDRES INIESTA

Barça's current captain moved to La Masia at the age of 12, and progressed through the youth ranks and B team to make his debut as an 18-year-old in 2002. His partnership with midfield general Xavi, and their shared understanding of Barça's style, was central to both Barcelona and Spain's success.

LIONEL MESSI

Leo's youth career started in Argentina with Newell's Old Boys, where he scored almost 500 goals for their 'Machine of '87' youth team, but he moved to Barcelona as a 13-year-old in 2001. In his first full season with the youth team, he scored 36 goals in just 30 games and became the star man in Barcelona's 'Baby Dream Team.' It wasn't long before he made his first-team debut, and he's now seen as La Masia's greatest ever graduate.

SERGIO BUSQUETS

Busquets joined La Masia in 2005, and within a few seasons became a key man in Guardiola's promotion-winning Barça B team of 2007-08. The following season, he stepped up to the first team alongside his boss, where his ability to keep the ball made him perfect for their midfield. He's since become a true Barcelona great.

JORDI ALBA

Barça-born pocket rocket Alba joined his hometown club in 1997, but was released aged 16. After progressing through the ranks at Valencia and being converted from a left winger to a left-back, he produced electric performances for Spain at Euro 2012 to convince his former club to re-sign him.

Levante v Barcelona in 2012

LA MASIA XI

Valdes

Montoya | Puyol | Pique | Alba

Busquets

Xavi | Fabregas

Pedro | Messi | Iniesta

Barcelona fielded this team of academy players in 2012 when Martin Montoya came on as a sub for Dani Alves!

ONES THAT GOT AWAY

CESC FABREGAS

Unlike Messi and Pique, Cesc accepted an offer from Arsenal at the age of 16. He returned home in 2011, but left Barcelona for a second time in 2014 to join Chelsea.

MAURO ICARDI

Icardi was at La Masia for three years, but was sold to Italian side Sampdoria for just £350,000 in 2011. He now has a £99 million release clause at Inter!

THIAGO ALCANTARA

Thiago made his Barcelona debut as an 18-year-old, and although he was expected to succeed Xavi in midfield, he followed Pep Guardiola to Bayern Munich in 2013.

MARC BARTRA

Bartra made his name in La Masia as a classy defender, but after failing to get into the first-team ahead of Pique and Mascherano, he joined Dortmund in 2016.

MIKEL ARTETA

Arteta only got to play for Barcelona B, before becoming a Premier League stalwart and part of Pep Guardiola's coaching set-up at Man. City.

PEPE REINA

The ex-Liverpool keeper played 30 league games for Barça as a teenager after graduating from La Masia, but eventually moved on in search of regular football.

HECTOR BELLERIN

Before becoming one of the Prem's best right-backs, Bellerin spent eight years at La Masia. He continues to be linked with a return to his hometown club.

SUAREZ
GOAL MACHINE

The Uruguay striker was the final piece of the MSN jigsaw.

In the summer of 2014, Barcelona needed something new. For the first time in six years, they ended the season trophyless and Messi also fell short of 30 league goals. With the arrival of new boss Luis Enrique, the club needed fresh blood to show that they were ready to return to the top. There was only one choice – the striker who'd just shared the European Golden Shoe with Cristiano Ronaldo. Fresh from firing Liverpool to within inches of the Premier League, Luis Suarez was the perfect signing, and not just because he had wanted to join Barcelona for many years. His work-rate and dribbling ability was as good as anyone's, but it was his goalscoring instincts and determination to run in behind defences that made him the ideal forward to complement Messi and Neymar. The club agreed to sign him for £65 million and MSN was born.

A LONG WAIT

A four-month ban following his bite on Giorgio Chiellini at the 2014 World Cup meant Suarez had to wait until October to make his debut in none other than El Clasico. For the first time, Messi, Suarez and Neymar started together, with the new boy beginning his Barça career on the right wing. His assist for the Brazilian inside five minutes didn't prevent a Real victory, but it did show that the magic between the trio had already begun.

TAKE OFF

The Uruguayan started his next couple of games from the right wing too, but after a 1-0 defeat to Celta Vigo doubts were creeping in. Sensing the problem during the next game against Ajax, Messi suggested to Suarez that they swap positions. The switch was a masterstroke. The No.9's movement and work-rate gave Leo the space to score two quality goals, and fire Los Cules to victory. The new-look front three was ready to dominate.

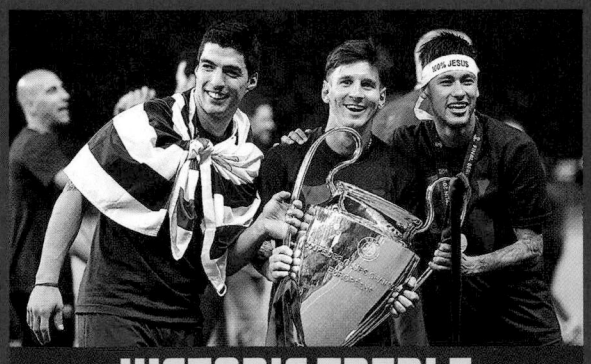

HISTORIC TREBLE

For the rest of the season, Barça only lost two games when MSN started together, and Suarez began to repay his transfer fee with some big goals. He fired home the winner when Real Madrid came to the Nou Camp, ended PSG's Champions League hopes with two goals in Paris and got on the score sheet against Juventus in the final. He ended the treble-winning season with 25 goals, as MSN reached a total of 122 strikes combined.

GOALS, GOALS, GOALS

The following season, Suarez was the focal point of the attack. He became the first player other than Messi and Ronaldo to win the Pichichi in six years, netting 40 times as Barça retained their La Liga trophy. In January 2017, he reached 100 goals for the club after just 120 games – the quickest player to do that since Laszlo Kubala in the 1950s. Whether he's creating goals for himself or his Barcelona team-mates, Suarez is a true goal machine.

BARÇA GOAL STATS

Total Goals: 121

La Liga Goals: 85

Champions League Goals: 18

Copa del Rey Goals: 11

Other Goals: 7

ICONIC KITS!

BARCELONA have had some awesome shirts during their history – check out some of the class Blaugrana strips of the past 50 years!

STAR MAN
Johan Cruyff
This iconic kit was magician Cruyff's first Barcelona strip!

HOME 1973-74

1973-74 wasn't just Barcelona's first La Liga title-winning campaign in 14 seasons, it marked a shift in how the club played football too. Led by Johan Cruyff, the Spanish giants showed others how the beautiful game should be played with jaw-dropping displays every week. They did it all in a top-quality kit, too!

DID YOU KNOW?
Everton gaffer Ronald Koeman scored the winning goal in the 1992 CL final!

AWAY 1991-92

This kit might look a bit crazy and eye-catching for some football purists, but it holds a special place in Barcelona fans' hearts. The Catalan club beat Italian giants Sampdoria in the orange strip to bag their first ever Champions League trophy, on top of winning another La Liga title. You can't argue with that!

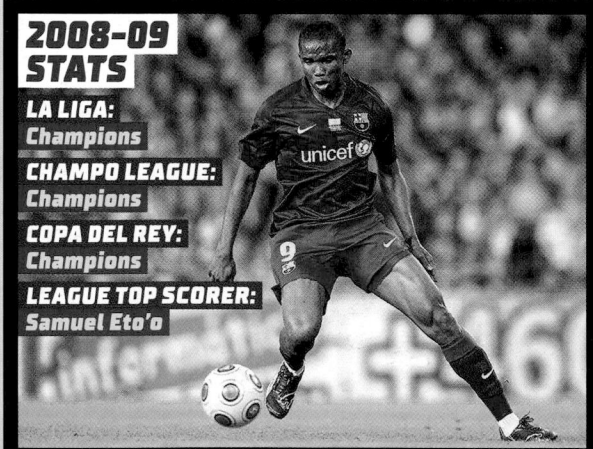

2008-09 STATS

LA LIGA:
Champions

CHAMPO LEAGUE:
Champions

COPA DEL REY:
Champions

LEAGUE TOP SCORER:
Samuel Eto'o

HOME 2008-09

The traditional Blaugrana stripes had gone in the 2008-09 season, but Barcelona's winning mentality certainly hadn't. In Pep Guardiola's first season in charge, Barça claimed the treble wearing this famous half-and-half shirt. 2009 was the year a certain Lionel Messi bagged his first Ballon d'Or, too!

DID YOU KNOW?
Barça won more La Liga games and scored more goals than Real during this season, but still failed to win the title!

AWAY 1996-97

Real Madrid pipped Barça to the La Liga title by just two points, but Catalan fans will still look back on this epic shirt with great memories. The club bagged the Copa del Rey, Cup Winners' Cup and Spanish Super Cup in 1996-97 and, in his only season at the club, Brazil legend Ronaldo hit 47 goals in 49 games!

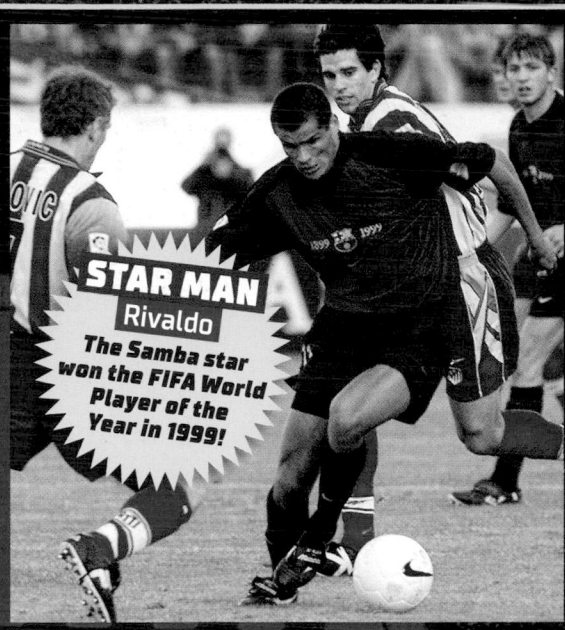

STAR MAN
Rivaldo
The Samba star won the FIFA World Player of the Year in 1999!

HOME 1998-99

When Barcelona were founded way back in 1899, the shirts they wore were half-and-half masterpieces. Fast forward 100 years, and Nike made this classic kit for the La Liga giants to celebrate their anniversary in. Not only did it look class, Barcelona won their sixth league title in nine years wearing it!

HOME 2014-15

AWAY 2013-14

This was another eye-popping kit in the club's history, but that didn't stop it being popular with Barça fans. It was the first shirt to feature Catalonia's red and yellow stripes, the region in Spain where the city is based. It was an instant classic among supporters, but the club wasn't very successful wearing it!

DID YOU KNOW?
Barça didn't win a major trophy for the first time in six years in 2013-14!

AWAY 2007-08

HOME 1997-98

FAB FACT
Barça lost just four games on their way to the 2004-05 La Liga title!

HOME 2004-05

A solid kit and a solid season for Barcelona, but the 2004-05 season was more about how the club would be changed forever after Lionel Messi made his La Liga debut. The legendary Argentine came on as an 82nd-minute substitute against local rivals Espanyol in October 2004 and, as they say, the rest is history!

THIRD 2002-03

DRAW YOUR BARÇA HERO!

BARCELONA have some of the best players on the planet, so why not sketch your favourite superstar for the chance to win a top prize?

BARÇA'S BEST BRAZILIAN!

Some of the most famous Brazilian footballers on the planet have played for BARCELONA. Here are the six best Samba superstars to ever wear the Blaugrana shirt!

6

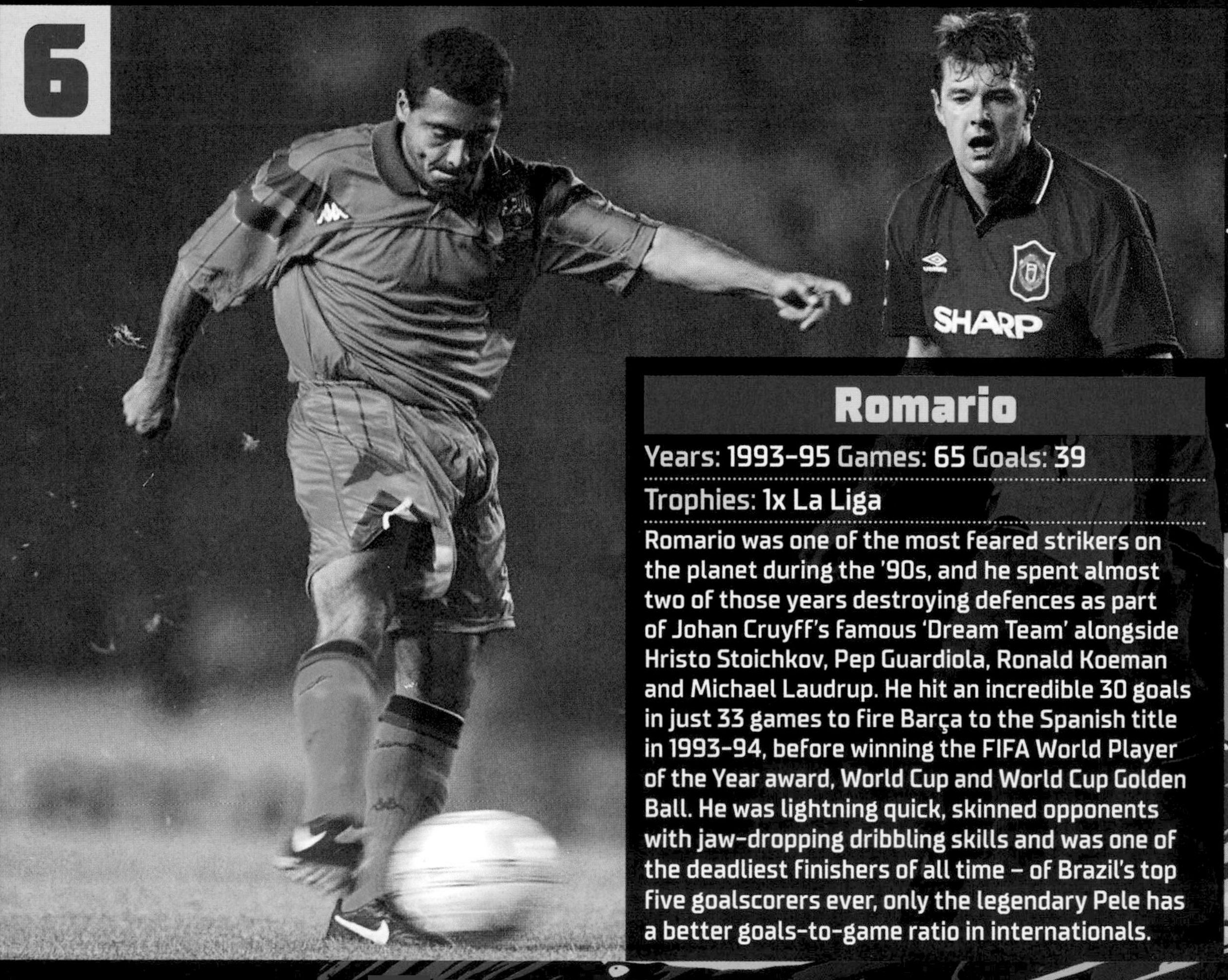

Romario

Years: 1993-95 Games: 65 Goals: 39

Trophies: 1x La Liga

Romario was one of the most feared strikers on the planet during the '90s, and he spent almost two of those years destroying defences as part of Johan Cruyff's famous 'Dream Team' alongside Hristo Stoichkov, Pep Guardiola, Ronald Koeman and Michael Laudrup. He hit an incredible 30 goals in just 33 games to fire Barça to the Spanish title in 1993-94, before winning the FIFA World Player of the Year award, World Cup and World Cup Golden Ball. He was lightning quick, skinned opponents with jaw-dropping dribbling skills and was one of the deadliest finishers of all time – of Brazil's top five goalscorers ever, only the legendary Pele has a better goals-to-game ratio in internationals.

5

Ronaldo

Years: 1996–97 **Games:** 49 **Goals:** 47

Trophies: 1x European Cup Winners' Cup, 1x Copa del Rey, 1x Spanish Super Cup

The original Ronaldo was hot property when he joined Barça as a 19-year-old for a world record £13.2 million in 1996. 'The Phenomenon' had it all – power, pace, ice-cool composure and a killer instinct. His most famous strike for the club – an incredible solo effort against Compostela, which saw him dribble all the way from his own half – is still remembered by fans today. But his one and only season at the Nou Camp was packed with so much more – he scored versus a record 19 La Liga opponents, won the Pichichi after bagging 34 goals in 37 games, hit the winner in the Cup Winners' Cup final and won both the FIFA World Player of the Year and European Golden Shoe awards.

4

Neymar

Years: 2013–2017 **Games:** 186 **Goals:** 105

Trophies: 1x Club World Cup, 1x Champions League, 1x European Super Cup, 2x La Ligas, 3x Copas del Rey, 2x Spanish Super Cups

One of the most skilful players of his generation, Neymar lit up the Nou Camp during his time in Spain and formed one third of MSN alongside Lionel Messi and Luis Suarez – the most lethal attack in football history. It took him just 177 games to hit 100 goals for the Catalan club – 11 games fewer than Messi, and he ripped net 39 times in all comps to help fire Barça to a famous treble in 2014-15. Neymar was quick, tricky, ultra intelligent and a deadly finisher, but he wasn't just about goals. The Samba star was a true icon on and off the pitch to Barcelona fans, and he captained Brazil to Olympic gold in 2016 to prove he was an inspirational leader too.

3

Dani Alves

Years: 2008-16 **Games:** 391 **Goals:** 21

Trophies: *3x Club World Cups, 3x Champions Leagues, 3x European Super Cups, 6x La Ligas, 4x Copas del Rey, 4x Spanish Super Cups, 2x Catalan Cups, 1x Catalan Super Cup*

Standing on the podium as the third best Brazilian in Barça's history is the only star in this list who's not an attacker. Flying full-back Alves' combination of raw power, solid defending, awesome energy and rocket shots means he's considered the best right-back in the club's history. Alves won an incredible 26 trophies during his eight-year spell at the Nou Camp – including two famous trebles – and was named La Liga's Best Defender in 2009. He's mostly remembered by Barcelona fans for two things – the crazy way he celebrated winning all of those trophies, and his mind-blowing partnership on the right wing with Lionel Messi – the only foreigner to play more games for Barcelona than Alves.

2

Rivaldo

Years: 1997-2002 **Games:** 235 **Goals:** 130

Trophies: 1x European Super Cup, 2x La Ligas, 1x Copa del Rey, 1x Catalan Cup

When Barça sold Ronaldo to Inter for a world record £19.5 million in 1997, little did they know his replacement would end up becoming an even bigger club legend. Rivaldo wasn't an out-and-out striker – he was a tall left winger with a rocket left foot – but that didn't stop him becoming Barça's all-time top-scoring Brazilian. Winning the Ballon d'Or and FIFA World Player of the Year award in 1999 cemented his place as the best player on the planet, and no Barça fan will ever forget his hat-trick against Valencia in 2001, which sealed Champions League football for the club. Two long-range screamers and an unbelievable overhead kick meant you had to see it to believe it!

1

Ronaldinho

Years: 2003-08 **Games:** 207 **Goals:** 94

Trophies: 1x Champions League, 2x La Ligas, 2x Spanish Super Cups, 3x Catalan Cups

A Barcelona's best ever Brazilians list could only ever be topped by one man. Ronaldinho became one of the greatest footballers of all time during his spell at the Nou Camp, and changed the club's history forever with his flair, trickery, assists and goals. Instantly recognisable thanks to his unique hairstyle and cheeky smile, Ronaldinho fired Barça to back-to-back La Liga titles and a first Champions League crown in 14 years. Not many players transcend clubs during their career, but the 2005 Ballon d'Or winner and 2x FIFA World Player of the Year did exactly that – he was loved by football fans all over the world, and even got a standing ovation from Real Madrid supporters after two wondergoals and an individual masterclass at The Bernabeu in 2005.

Stats only include official matches. Correct up to the start of the 2017-18 season.

PIQUE
MR. CATALONIA

If Andres Iniesta is Barcelona's brain, Gerard Pique is its heart.

Gerard Pique has Barça in his blood. The defender was born and raised a fan of his hometown club, and his grandfather even served as vice-president. It seems impossible he could ever have wanted to leave, but when Man. United called in 2004, he took the chance to move abroad. In four seasons there, he grew from a boy to a man, adding English strength and physicality to his Catalan passing and skill. He returned to the Nou Camp in November 2006, but on the subs' bench of Real Zaragoza, where he was spending the season on loan. His 22 La Liga games that year convinced Barça to re-sign him, and in 2008, with Pep Guardiola in charge, Pique came home. He has gone on to become one of the most decorated players in world football, but most importantly for Barça fans, the boyhood fan and local lad is still one of their own.

DEFENSIVE MASTER

While Pep Guardiola's teams always seemed to dazzle with their incisive attacking play, it's easy to forget just how good their defensive record was – and Pique was central to that. After he re-joined the Catalan club, Barça had the best defence in La Liga for the next four seasons in a row. His La Masia education allowed him to pass as well as a midfielder, and his ability to retain possession and start attacks made him a star.

TROPHY COLLECTOR

Pique has picked up a trophy in almost every season since returning to the Nou Camp, and there aren't many competitions he hasn't won. He knows how to celebrate them, too – after the 2011 Champions League Final, the defender clambered onto the Wembley crossbar and cut down the net in tribute to the traditions of Barcelona's basketball team. His iconic net-cutting habit has continued as he's gone on to rack up the trophies.

THE WIND-UP MASTER

One thing that marks out Pique's popularity at the Nou Camp is his unpopularity with Real Madrid supporters. The defender never misses a chance to make fun of Barcelona's rivals – even his international centre-back partner Sergio Ramos. The pair have clashed loads of times, but Pique usually comes out on top – he's won ten of his 15 La Liga El Clasico appearances, and even scored in the famous 6-2 win at The Bernabeu in 2009.

HEART OF THE TEAM

After the retirement of legendary centre-back Carles Puyol in 2014, Pique took over the role as Barcelona's senior centre-back and the city's representative on the pitch. With nine appearances for Catalonia, he is an ambassador for the region and has even been jeered while on international duty for Spain due to his pro-Catalonia stance. His role for Barcelona helps to make it 'Mes que un club' – more than a club.

BARÇA TROPHY CABINET

3x Champions Leagues

6x La Ligas

3x Club World Cups

5x Copas del Rey

5x Spanish Super Cups

3x European Super Cups

WORDFIT

Can you fit the Barcelona legends into the giant grid below?

GUARDIOLA

Abidal	Cruyff	Koeman	Pedro	Ronaldo
Bakero	Czibor	Kubala	Puyol	Samitier
Basora	Enrique	Maradona	Quini	Stoichkov
Begiristain	Gamper	Migueli	Ramallets	Valdes
Cesar	Guardiola	Neeskens	Rexach	Xavi
Comamala	Kocsis	Olivella	Romario	Zubizarreta

NAME THE TEAM

stars from Barça's Champions League clash with Man. City
the Nou Camp are hidden – can you work out who they are?

1. Goalkeeper

2. Right-back

3. Centre-back

5. Defensive midfielder

6. Centre-back

Legends o
m all out...

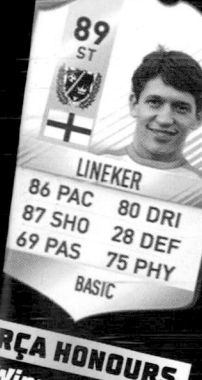

8. Forward

9. Attacking midfielder

11. Left-back

BARCELONA'S
ALL-TIME FU
LEGENDS

With the release of brand-new FUT Icons on FIFA 18
check out what made some past BARCELONA L
FIFA's Ultimate Team so legendary! Check ther

LINEKER

1986-89
Games: 137 ★ Goals: 52

Gary Lineker was one of the world's best goal poachers. The last Englishman to play for Barcelona signed after winning the Golden Boot at the 1986 World Cup, and became a fans' favourite after scoring a hat-trick in El Clasico!

BA
Cup
Copa

STOICHKOV

1990-95 & 1996-98
Games: 336 ★ Goals: 162

The Barça side assembled by Johan Cruyff in the '90s was known as 'The Dream Team', and Hristo Stoichkov was its star. The Bulgarian played with freedom, and was worshipped by the fans for his talent, fighting spirit and love for the club!

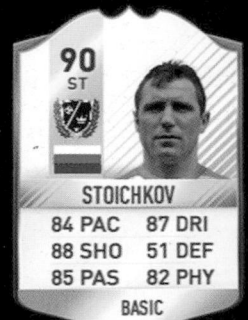

90
ST
STOICHKOV
84 PAC 87 DRI
88 SHO 51 DEF
85 PAS 82 PHY
BASIC

BARÇA HONOURS
Champions League	1
La Liga	5
Cup Winners' Cup	1
Copa del Rey	2
UEFA Super Cup	2
Spanish Super Cup	4

LAUDRUP

1989-94
Games: 288 ★ Goals: 93

Michael Laudrup's passing, dribbling and vision helped Barça to a European Cup and four La Liga titles in a row. However, after being left out of the 1994 CL Final, the Denmark ace completed a highly controversial move to arch rivals Real Madrid!

89
CAM
L
85 PA
73 SH
87 PAS

BARÇA
Champions
La Liga
UEFA Supe
Copa del R
Spanish Su

...IVERT

...8-2004
...255 ★ Goals: 120

Signed by Louis van Gaal, Patrick Kluivert was one of five Holland stars to join Barça in the same season. His partnership with Rivaldo fired The Catalans to the title in his first season, and made him one of the most feared No.9s in Europe!

88
ST

KLUIVERT

86 PAC	82 DRI
86 SHO	41 DEF
80 PAS	81 PHY

BASIC

BARÇA HONOURS
| La Liga | 1 |

DE BOER

1999-2003
Games: 215 ★ Goals: 15

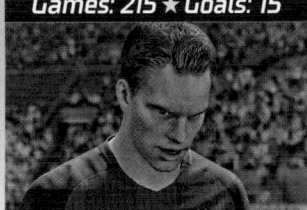

Frank de Boer joined Barça with twin brother Ronald for £22 million. The left-footed defender's passing ability from the back was key to Barça's possession football, and his shooting made him a threat from penalties and free-kicks!

86
CB

DE BOER

66 PAC	65 DRI
61 SHO	88 DEF
79 PAS	78 PHY

BASIC

BARÇA HONOURS
| La Liga | 1 |

FIGO

1995-2000
Games: 249 ★ Goals: 45

Luis Figo would be one of Barcelona's all-time greats if he hadn't committed the ultimate sin of joining Real Madrid. The winger was one of the most exciting dribblers ever seen at the club, and won plenty of trophies at the Nou Camp!

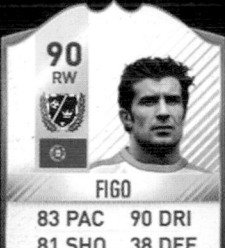

90
RW

FIGO

83 PAC	90 DRI
81 SHO	38 DEF
86 PAS	75 PHY

BASIC

BARÇA HONOURS
La Liga	2
Cup Winners' Cup	1
Copa del Rey	2
UEFA Super Cup	1
Spanish Super Cup	1

DECO

2004-08
Games: 188 ★ Goals: 28

After winning the 2004 CL with Porto, Deco became the heartbeat in manager Frank Rijkaard's new-look Barça team. Alongside Ronaldinho, he provided the creative spark behind two La Liga titles in a row and the 2006 CL crown!

87
CAM

DECO

83 PAC	88 DRI
78 SHO	39 DEF
89 PAS	68 PHY

BASIC

BARÇA HONOURS
Champions League	1
La Liga	2
Spanish Super Cup	2

LARSSON

2004-06
Games: 58 ★ Goals: 19

The Celtic legend's Barça career was blighted by injury, but he left the Nou Camp a hero. With Barça trailing Arsenal by a goal in the 2006 CL Final, Larsson came off the bench to bag two assists, and bring the trophy back to Catalonia!

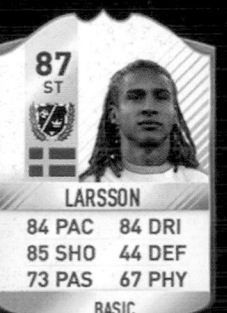

87
ST

LARSSON

84 PAC	84 DRI
85 SHO	44 DEF
73 PAS	67 PHY

BASIC

BARÇA HONOURS
Champions League	1
La Liga	2
Spanish Super Cup	1

BARCELONA'S TOP 10 EL CLASICO MOMENTS!

Get a load of some of BARÇA's best ever moments against arch rivals Real Madrid!

ENGLISH EL CLASICO!
Barcelona 3–2 Real Madrid
La Liga, 1987

One of the Catalan club's greatest ever wins against Real was orchestrated by two Englishmen. Three Lions legend Gary Lineker was the star of the show, scoring an epic treble to put Real to the sword. The man in charge of Barcelona? Ex-England manager Terry Venables!

9 MESSI MAGIC!
Barcelona 3–3 Real Madrid
La Liga, 2007

2006–07 was Leo Messi's real breakthrough season, and this game proved it. Three times Barcelona went behind, and three times Messi came to their rescue. His quality hat-trick included a trademark solo goal!

6 SOLO STUNNER!
Real Madrid 0–2 Barcelona
Champions League, 2011

This tight CL semi-final first leg looked like it was heading for a 0-0 draw, but Messi had other ideas! The Argentina megastar scored twice in the last 15 minutes, including one of the great Clasico goals. Leo took the ball just inside the Real half, beat four defenders and rolled the ball home!

8 LEO WHO?
Real Madrid 0–4 Barcelona
La Liga, 2015

Barça proved they weren't a one-man team when Messi was injured for El Clasico in 2015. Luis Suarez bagged twice, Neymar dazzled with his skills and Andres Iniesta was given a standing ovation for his performance!

COOL CRUYFF!
Real Madrid 0–5 Barcelona
La Liga, 1974

7

In the early '70s, Barça had around half the league titles of rivals Real, so something needed to change. Step forward Johan Cruyff! The Holland magician fired Barça to their first La Liga title in 14 years – and scored one and set up three in this thumping Clasico win!

TREBLE TROUBLE!
Real Madrid 3-4 Barcelona
La Liga, 2014

Another Messi hat-trick decided El Clasico, and he went past Alfredo Di Stefano's all-time Clasico goals record in the process. Two late Leo penalties sent the Barcelona fans at The Bernabeu into a frenzy!

5.

4

REAL HIT FOR SIX!
Real Madrid 2-6 Barcelona
La Liga, 2009

One of Real's worst ever Clasico defeats marked a shift in power in Spain. Pep Guardiola's Barça played beautiful footy in this huge win, with Messi and Thierry Henry both scoring twice. They would dominate football for years to come!

MANITA OVER MOURINHO!
Barcelona 5-0 Real Madrid
La Liga, 2010

3

Jose Mourinho's first El Clasico as Real boss was one to forget – he described it the 'worst defeat' of his career. The 5-0 thrashing, La Manita in Spanish, was summed up by Barça's second goal, where the home side scored after 22 consecutive passes!

1

LEO DOES IT AGAIN!
Real Madrid 2-3 Barcelona
La Liga, 2017

Another Clasico – cue more Messi magic! The game was heading for a draw, with Real getting an all-important point in their quest for the title. Leo had other ideas, though. The Barça legend fired home from the edge of the box in injury-time to take his side to the top of the table and bring up his 500th Barça goal. His shirt-showing celebration is well iconic!

2

RONALDINHO RUNS THE SHOW!
Real Madrid 0-3 Barcelona
La Liga, 2005

Real fans rarely give their own stars a standing ovation, so when a Barça player gets one, you know they've done something special. 2005 Ballon d'Or winner Ronaldinho got applauded at The Bernabeu for his individual masterclass!

MESSI
RECORD BREAKER

The records just keep on tumbling!

Every year, it seems Lionel Messi breaks records. Whether he's overtaking a top goalscorer or racking up another trophy, Leo's numbers are frightening, and keep on getting better. Take a look at some of his most impressive achievements...

INDIVIDUAL RECORDS

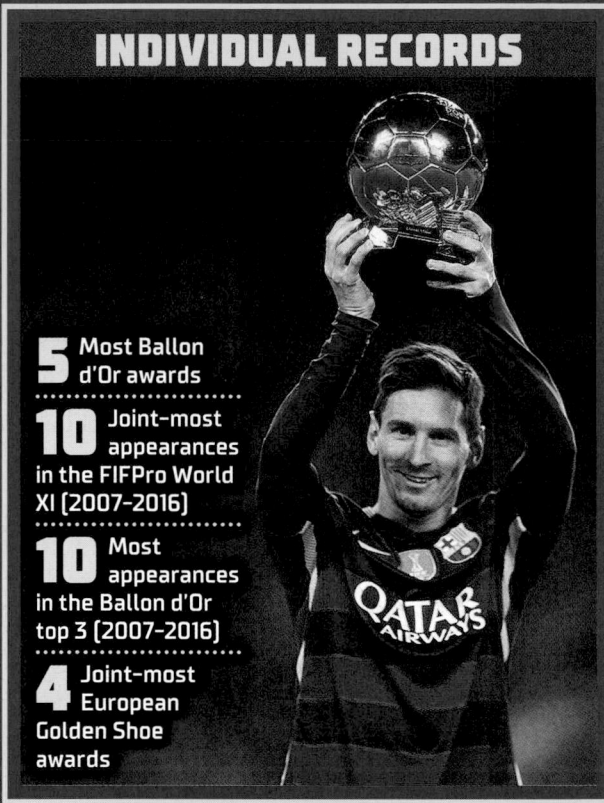

5 Most Ballon d'Or awards

10 Joint-most appearances in the FIFPro World XI [2007-2016]

10 Most appearances in the Ballon d'Or top 3 [2007-2016]

4 Joint-most European Golden Shoe awards

BARCELONA RECORDS

507 All-time top goalscorer

97 Top goalscorer in European club competitions

23 Most goals in El Clasico

LA LIGA RECORDS

349 Most goals

50 Most goals in a season

135 Most assists

WORLD RECORDS

91 Most goals in a calendar year, set in 2012

1 Only player to score 40+ club goals in eight seasons in a row

21 Most league matches scored in a row – 33 goals in total

MESSI BOOT HISTORY

adidas gave LIONEL MESSI his own signature boots back in 2008. We take a look at some of his best kicks since then!

2008: *F50.9 TUNIT Messi*
When Barça demolished Real Madrid 6-2, Messi laced-up in these cleats!

2009: *F50i TUNIT Messi*
Leo has fond memories of the F50i – he scored four past Arsenal in them!

2010: *F50 adizero Messi Ballon d'Or*
Of course, the reigning world POTY had to get a gold pair of F50 adizeros!

2011: *F50 adizero Messi Ballon d'Or*
Three Ballons d'Or got Messi a pair of these white and gold bad boys!

2013: *F50 adizero Messi Ballon d'Or*
Yep, another Ballon d'Or and another pair of epic gold-trimmed boots!

2014: *F50 adizero Messi Turbo Blast*
Messi slipped these eye-busters on to score a hat-trick in El Clasico!

2014: *F50 adizero Messi Battle Pack*
2014 World Cup final losing cleats... look away now, Messi. Sorry, Leo!

2014: *F50 adizero Messi Neon Orange*
Back to better times, and the boots worn to beat La Liga's scoring record!

2015: *F50 adizero Messi P. de Barr10*
Messi's last ever F50 kicks were a tribute to his hometown in Argentina.

2015: *MESSI 15.1*
adidas gave Lionel not only his own colourway, but a boot just for him!

2016: *MESSI 16.1*
adidas released these next-gen Leo kicks before the 2016 Copa America!

2016: *MESSI 16.1*
Loads of footy-mad fans loved the gradient on these when they dropped!

2017: *MESSI 16.1*
His 500th Barça goal was bagged in
El Clasico in these. Legendary boots!

2017: *Messi Nemeziz 17.1*
Leo kicked off the 2017-18 season
wearing the all-new Nemeziz cleats!

2017-18 FIRST TEAM SQUAD

GOALKEEPERS

No.	Player	La Liga Games/Goals 2016-17	Signed from
1	Marc-A. Ter Stegen	36/0	B. M'gladbach, 2014
13	Jasper Cillessen	1/0	Ajax, 2016

Jasper Cillessen

DEFENDERS

No.	Player	La Liga Games/Goals 2016-17	Signed from
2	Nelson Semedo	N/A	Benfica, 2017
3	Gerard Pique	25/2	Man. United, 2008
14	Javier Mascherano	25/1	Liverpool, 2010
18	Jordi Alba	26/1	Valencia, 2012
19	Lucas Digne	17/0	PSG, 2016
22	Aleix Vidal	6/2	Sevilla, 2015
23	Samuel Umtiti	25/1	Lyon, 2016
	Thomas Vermaelen	N/A	Arsenal, 2014

Gerard Pique

MIDFIELDERS

No.	Player	La Liga Games/Goals 2016-17	Signed from
4	Ivan Rakitic	32/8	Sevilla, 2014
5	Sergio Busquets	33/0	Academy
6	Denis Suarez	26/1	Villarreal, 2016
7	Arda Turan	18/3	Atletico, 2015
8	Andres Iniesta	23/0	Academy
12	Rafinha	18/6	Academy
15	Paulinho	NA	Guangzhou, 2017
20	Sergi Roberto	32/0	Academy
21	Andre Gomes	30/3	Valencia, 2016

Ousmane Dembele

FORWARDS

No.	Player	La Liga Games/Goals 2016-17	Signed from
9	Luis Suarez	35/29	Liverpool, 2014
10	Lionel Messi	34/37	Academy
11	Ousmane Dembele	N/A	Dortmund, 2017
16	Gerard Deulofeu	N/A	Everton, 2017
17	Paco Alcacer	20/6	Valencia, 2016

ERNESTO VALVERDE

Country: Spain

D.O.B: 9 February, 1964

Former Club: Athletic Bilbao

Honours: 1x Spanish Super Cup, 3x Greece Superleague

After Luis Enrique announced his departure towards the end of 2016-17, Barcelona's bosses went in search of a new manager that ticked all the boxes. They wanted somebody with a proven track record, that understood the club, and could produce the kind of beautiful football the Nou Camp faithful are used to.

They found just the man in Ernesto Valverde. The Athletic Bilbao gaffer built an impressive side on the north coast of Spain, and had serious experience to back him up. As well as spells in charge of Espanyol, Villarreal and Valencia, the Spaniard spent three seasons in Greece with Superleague giants Olympiakos, winning the title every year.

More importantly, he knows all about Barcelona. The former La Liga goal machine spent two seasons at the Nou Camp under Johan Cruyff, and was tipped for greatness by his ex-manager. If Valverde can come close to his mentor's success, he'll become a hero to the Blaugrana fans.

Wordsearch — P14

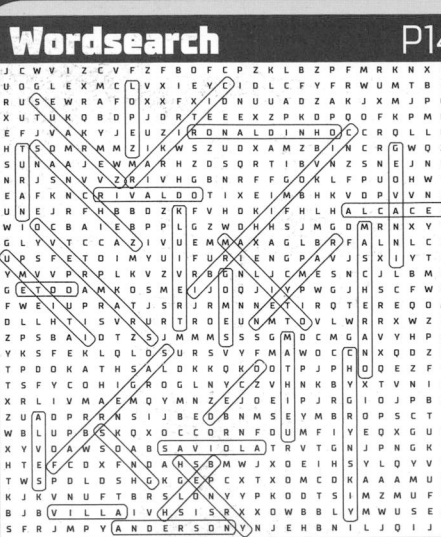

Brain-Buster — P30

1. 2002
2. German
3. Over 90,000
4. Five
5. Liverpool
6. 11
7. Midfield
8. Blue
9. Neymar
10. Espanyol

Name The Team — P49

1. Marc-Andre ter Stegen
2. Javier Mascherano
3. Samuel Umtiti
4. Ivan Rakitic
5. Sergio Busquets
6. Gerard Pique
7. Lionel Messi
8. Neymar
9. Andres Iniesta
10. Luis Suarez
11. Jordi Alba

Spot The Difference — P15

Wordfit — P48

Face In The Crowd — P31

FREE ISSUE OF MATCH! FOR EVERY READER!

PACKED EVERY WEEK WITH...

★ Red-hot gear
★ FIFA tips
★ Stats & facts
★ Massive stars
★ Quizzes & pics
& loads more!

TO CLAIM YOUR FREE COPY OF MATCH...
CALL 0800 923 3006 QUOTE: MATT100

ROLL OF HONOUR

CHAMPIONS LEAGUE
1991-92, 2005-06, 2008-09, 2010-11, 2014-15

FIFA CLUB WORLD CUP
2009, 2011, 2015

EUROPEAN CUP WINNERS' CUP
1978-79, 1981-82, 1988-89, 1996-97

FAIRS CUP
1957-58, 1959-60, 1965-66 (won outright in 1971)

EUROPEAN SUPER CUP
1992, 1997, 2009, 2011, 2015

LA LIGA
1928-29, 1944-45, 1947-48, 1948-49, 1951-52,
1952-53, 1958-59, 1959-60, 1973-74, 1984-85,
1990-91, 1991-92, 1992-93, 1993-94, 1997-98,
1998-99, 2004-05, 2005-06, 2008-09,
2009-10, 2010-11, 2012-13, 2014-15, 2015-16

COPA DEL REY
1909-10, 1911-12, 1912-13, 1919-20, 1921-22,
1924-25, 1925-26, 1927-28, 1941-42, 1950-51,
1951-52, 1952-53, 1956-57, 1958-59, 1962-63,
1967-68, 1970-71, 1977-78, 1980-81, 1982-83,
1987-88, 1989-90, 1996-97, 1997-98, 2008-09,
2011-12, 2014-15, 2015-16, 2016-17

SPANISH SUPER CUP
1983, 1991, 1992, 1994, 1996, 2005, 2006, 2009,
2010, 2011, 2013, 2016

SPANISH LEAGUE CUP
1982-83, 1985-86

SMALL WORLD CUP
1957

LATIN CUP
1949, 1952

PYRENEES CUP
1910, 1911, 1912, 1913

MEDITERRANEAN LEAGUE
1937

CATALAN LEAGUE
1937-38

CATALAN LEAGUE CHAMPIONSHIP
1901-02, 1902-03, 1904-05, 1908-09, 1909-10,
1910-11, 1912-13, 1915-16, 1918-19, 1919-20,
1920-21, 1921-22, 1923-24, 1924-25, 1925-26,
1926-27, 1927-28, 1929-30, 1930-31, 1931-32,
1934-35, 1935-36, 1937-38 (includes Copa
Macaya 1901-02 and Copa Barcelona 1902-03)

CATALAN SUPER CUP
2014-15

CATALAN CUP
1990-91, 1992-93, 1999-2000, 2003-04,
2004-05, 2006-07, 2012-13, 2013-14
(until 1993-94, Copa Generalitat)

EVA DUARTE CUP
1948-49, 1951-52, 1952-53